READERS AND REVIEWERS ARE SAYING—

"THE OTHER SIDE OF WELCOME *is the other side of the coin. Sue Ellen Johnson has used all of her considerable writing skills to draw a portrait of modern Israel you may not recognize. The country and its problems are seen through the eyes, and in the voice, of Father Chacour, a prominent educator who is both a Palestinian and a Christian."*

Mike McGrady
Former *Newsday New York* critic and author
Lilliwaup, Washington

"This book tells a powerful and moving story about the life of a remarkable person, living in a very turbulent time and place. Young readers will have a new door of understanding opened for them as the life and times of Father Chacour unfolds before them. It is sure to be both informative and inspiring reading."

The Reverend James C. Killough
St. Timothy's Lutheran Church
Omaha, Nebraska

"This historical biography is a most balanced and lucid account of a virtually forgotten people, the Christian Palestinians, and has a true hero, Elias Chacour. It is well suited for contemporary adolescents who are too often swayed by the materialism and false values of super athletes and entertainers. It makes the reader aware of both individual and group struggles in a land where so many cultures and religions intersect. It offers hope for the solution to centuries-old problems, if only we respect differences and have faith."

Dr. Barbara Godbold
Teacher/Traveler/Anthropologist/Editor
Brick, New Jersey

"This history of the Israeli/Palestinian conflict is brought to light through the unique perspective and thought provoking story of Elias Chacour's life. Young adults will gain a truly human understanding of the complicated nature of this region and its diverse peoples."

Kristin M. Storey
Middle School Social Studies Teacher
Seattle, Washington

"My sons, ages ten and thirteen, and I ⎯⎯ *THER SIDE OF WELCOME together and found it to be a stimulus for family discussi⎯* ⎯⎯ *⎯blems. The engrossing story held their attention and offered them a youngst⎯* ⎯⎯ *⎯ the ⎯⎯⎯ East."*

Journal
Washington

"Mrs. Johnson takes her readers on a journey into the life ⎯ ⎯⎯ *⎯tian man who has lived his faith in a land of turmoil and unfortunate hostilities. Young readers ⎯* ⎯ *⎯n insight into the formation of the state of Israel and the "tables-turned" situation regarding present-day Jews and Palestinians. This book would be a welcome addition to school libraries and bookstores and would certainly be useful for supplemental reading in high school history classes. Mrs. Johnson presents a view of the Middle East from a gentler slant that is often neglected or overlooked altogether by the news media."*

Carol Abbott
Bordeaux School Librarian
Shelton, Washington

"The Other Side of Welcome *may appear to be small on the bookshelf at just 91 pages, but it will quickly gain a very large place in the reader's heart. Through the beautifully told story of Father Elias Chacour, author Sue Ellen Johnson brings the reader into the clash between those who believe the land belongs to them and the Palestinian people who believe "they belong to the land." Thanks to the author, media reports will no longer suffice to inform of events in the Holy Land. For, through her 'little' book, the faith-affirming and hope-filled story of Father Chacour and his family bring alive the people of the land who will long be remembered by the reader."*

The Reverend Donald A. Cornell, Board
Member of Evangelicals for Middle East
Understanding, Union, Washington

"*After reading* The Other Side of Welcome, *I have new insight regarding the historical framework of the Israeli/Palestinian conflict. This inspirational biography of Elias Chacour, who has lived out his faith under unbelievable circumstances, has helped me understand what it is like to live under occupation. I don't remember ever reading a book that affected me like this one. I can still recall the deep humility of Elias's father when he refused to hate those who had taken his land."*

Janna Wood, Evergreen School
Librarian, Shelton, Washington

The OTHER SIDE of WELCOME

SUE ELLEN JOHNSON

FIRST EDITION, SECOND PRINTING

RED APPLE PUBLISHING
Gig Harbor, WA 98329

Printed by Gorham Printing
Rochester, WA 98579

ISBN 1-880222-30-2

Library of Congress Catalog Card Number 97-76423

Cover design, by Kathryn E. Campbell, taken from the Gymnasium Mural at Prophet Elias College, Ibillin, Israel. Dianne Roe, artist.

DEDICATION

THIS BOOK IS DEDICATED TO CARL, *my husband and partner in peacemaking, as we seek to "Let justice roll down like waters and righteousness like an ever-flowing stream."* —AMOS 5:24

INTRODUCTION

THE OTHER SIDE OF WELCOME tells about the life of Elias Chacour. At his request, it is written as if he were telling the story.

At the present time, Abuna (Father) Chacour still lives in the village of Ibillin which is quite close to Nazareth, in Israel/Palestine. He is the administrator of Prophet Elias Secondary School and College. Abuna Chacour and the college were both named after the Old Testament prophet Elijah, who dedicated his life to doing God's will in the face of severe persecution. Abuna Chacour also travels around the world speaking at conferences and telling the story of his people, the Palestinians. He works tirelessly for peace for all people: Israelis and Palestinians, Christians, Jews and Muslims.

The author and Abuna Chacour on the balcony of Prophet Elias Secondary School.
December 1992

CONTENTS

1

PEACE GLADLY SHARED

Excitement charged the hot, dry air. The quiet rhythm of family and worship was somehow off balance. I could not tell just what was different, but I knew something had burst into my world. Father would know, I thought. I would ask him when the family gathered for the evening meal.

From the outdoor fire came the sweet smell of bread baking. I saw mother stooping over the metal oven which rested on a low grate beside the house. She looked up.

"Elias, your brother needs help carrying the water."

At seven, I only helped with small chores. Mother liked to pamper me, her youngest, and I didn't mind at all.

Our house, in the upper region of Galilee, was surrounded by the beauty of the Palestinian hills. The knowledge that My Champion, Jesus, had also walked these paths filled me with joy. Mother often drew me onto her lap and recounted wonderful Bible stories—stories that had taken place long ago in these very hills. These stories about Jesus touched the deep places within my spirit. My sister Wadi and brothers Atallah, Musah, Rudah and Chacour also listened with keen interest.

Mother's Bible stories and the jingle of her wedding necklace brought comfort and peace to me as a child, and that memory re-mained with me as I grew into manhood. The magical necklace, a wedding gift from Father, was a simple chain of tiny brass links from which dangled fish and doves. The fish represented fish caught by the Apostle Peter in the Sea of Galilee, and the doves represented the Holy Spirit. On hearing the jingle of this necklace, I knew Mother was near and all was well in my world.

When the family gathered in the courtyard for the evening meal, Mother said, "Elias, do you want to hear a story that I found under a stone in the field today?" As her gentle voice told of Jesus, searching these very hills for a lost sheep or leading His disciples down to the Sea of Galilee, I pictured our Lord drawing near this small village of Biram. Oh, the wonder of those peaceful family times together.

My mind wandered from the familiar story as I searched beyond the courtyard, waiting for Father's return. He often went to other villages to barter the figs and olives from our orchard for other things that were needed. Sometimes he went to neighboring Jewish villages to trade, stopping for the traditional *cup of friendship*. This tar-like, bittersweet coffee was the gesture of welcome between Arab and Jew alike, neighbors who lived together in God's holy land.

Although our family had but eight members, I felt the kinship of the other households in the village. All together we were one family under God. We all lived simply, raising the food that was part of our diet and occasionally bartering for other necessities. Meat was only eaten at certain times during the year. The Easter season brought a special treat. A lamb was slaughtered, and eating the roasted meat was a powerful reminder of Jesus, the Lamb of God, whose life was given as payment for our sins.

On this night Father was later than usual. When he arrived, he was leading a lamb. I eagerly rushed to meet him. Father was of slight stature, but a giant in our eyes. His hair and thick mustache of light brown were tinged with gray. Michael Chacour, at the age of fifty, was respected by his children and was a leader in the village. He radiated a mystical calmness that assured those who knew him that he was a man of peace.

"Elias, why are you so excited? Has a bird told you the news about our welcoming celebration? This lamb is soon to provide food for our special feast."

In the chill evening air we children clustered together around the fire as Mother handed out steaming plates of food. Father set his plate down so he could tell about the coming celebration. His words touched our hearts. He told about the terrible events that had taken place in Europe. An evil leader, Hitler, had been killing Jews: men, women and children. These people were killed only because they were Jews. They had done no wrong.

Tears sprang to my eyes as I thought of the Jewish families I knew. Would they die, too?

Father continued. "Many Jews have left their homes, and even though Hitler is dead, they cannot return. They are frightened and homeless. Some of them are coming here to make a new home. That is why we will have a celebration to welcome them to their new home. We will celebrate the Resurrection early in honor of our Jewish brothers and sisters who are alive and have escaped from Hitler's threat of death. The first to come will be Jewish soldiers called Zionists. They will carry machine guns, but we must not be afraid. They come in peace."

What a puzzle this news was for me. The Zionists would come in peace but would carry guns. "Where will they stay, Father? When will they come?"

Father looked weary as he gently explained that the family would move up to the roof. Then the soldiers would have a comfortable place to stay and would know we welcome them. Although spring nights were cool, we could bundle up and be warm enough. On hot summer nights we often slept on the roof, hoping to catch a cool breeze. Never before had we gone up in spring. As I thought of Father's news, my eyelids soon became heavy and I snuggled into Mother's protective arms, totally forgetting my second question. As I drifted off to sleep, I heard Father's comforting voice leading us in evening prayers.

2

WELCOME BETRAYED

This land of Palestine had been home to the Chacour family for centuries. As Arabs, we had shared our colorful history, both joys and sorrows, with the Jews of Palestine, down through the ages. Now, in the twentieth century, Father brought the past to life with stories of Chacour ancestors. Intertwined with these stories, he wove the teachings of Jesus. The Melkite Church, which traced its beginnings to James, the brother of Jesus, was a focal point of village life. Father lived out Jesus's teachings as he willingly forgave those who took advantage of him and then prayed that God would send them blessings. His advice was frequently sought by the village mukhtars, or leaders.

Time seemed to stand still as we waited for the Zionists. Word came to the village mukhtars that when the soldiers came they would stay only a few days. Their mission was to check out the land. They promised to take nothing.

Although Father had assured us that the soldiers came in peace, my brother Rudah was not convinced. One night he brought home a rifle—"for protection," he said.

Kind and gentle Father was horrified. In anger he shouted at Rudah, "Get it out of here! I won't have it in my house!" Then patiently he explained that Jews and Palestinians are brothers and have shared this land for centuries. "We cannot welcome these homeless brothers with a rifle in our hands. After all,

Abraham was the father of both of our people." (That ancestry can be traced to about 2200 years before Christ, 2200 B.C.) Together, Father and Rudah disposed of the rifle.

Then they came. Two weeks later the village awoke to the rumble of trucks and jeeps. Father welcomed these soldier-guests with the lamb killed and prepared for the welcoming feast. The soldiers ate with gusto, the guns glinting coldly by their sides. They moved on into the village as villagers quietly stepped aside to let them pass.

Whenever possible, village life went on as usual. Children went to school and mothers moved through their daily routines. The village men quietly tended their flocks and orchards. At night, families slept under the chill of spring starlight, huddled on their roofs, while the soldiers stomped around below in their homes and courtyards. Each day the villagers were sure this would be the day that the soldiers moved on.

After about a week, the military commander arrived, bringing *confidential news*. He told us that for our own safety we should leave our homes and move out into the hills. The soldiers would protect the village from any trouble between the ruling British and the Zionists. Dismayed, we turned over the keys to our homes and, with whatever belongings we could carry, fled to a grove of olive trees outside of the village. The streets were overflowing with families and friends, all fleeing to safety, leaving our beloved village of Biram to the protection of the soldiers. As we left, Father uttered a prayer that God would protect our homes, and the soldiers, too.

At first, camping in the olive grove was an adventure. As the days wore on, the rocky ground made sleeping difficult. The hot sunny days and damp cold nights caused sickness, especially among the oldest and the youngest. Finally, the village elders decided to go back and find out how much longer we must wait.

The report they brought back filled us with fear. On entering Biram they had found doors broken in and the contents of their homes smashed to pieces. They were stopped by rough soldiers who told them that the commander had gone and these homes belonged, not to the villagers, but to the soldiers. Once more the people fled to the olive groves, this time with the soldiers' words ringing in their ears. "Move! This land is ours. Get out now!"

What could be done? The mukhtars decided together that we should move on to the neighboring village of Gish. Perhaps these kind brothers would give us shelter until this problem could be solved. And so we went.

Entering Gish, we were met with silence. There was no friendly welcome, as we had expected. To our surprise, only ten elders were in the village. They told how soldiers had come and driven the villagers away at gun point. One old man said shots rang out, scaring the people as they left the village. The elders extended a welcome to the people from Biram, and soon all of us had found housing. Some families were cramped in small quarters but there was no choice. Temporarily, this would protect them from the sun and rain.

The boys, glad to be somewhat settled, forgot the horrors of days past and ran off to play soccer in the village sand lot. As I chased a ball, I stumbled on something sticking out of the ground. I tried to pull it up and then jumped back in fear. It was a boy's arm. My cries soon brought the other boys and then their parents.

In shock they dug, only to find a shallow grave. There were about two dozen villagers from Gish buried here. Now the truth was known. All of the people of Gish had not fled to safety. Some were the targets of those warning shots that the elders had heard.

I tried to forget this day of horror. Some villagers spoke of revenge, but Father and others counseled for peace.

Meanwhile, in 1947 the "question of Palestine" had come before the United Nations (U.N.). This world supreme court of justice was about to make a decision that would leave Palestinians without a homeland or an identity. The Zionists were to replace the British as the ruling power, just as the British had replaced the Ottoman Turks about 400 years earlier when the

Ottoman Empire fell in 1453. Throughout the centuries, ruling powers have come and gone. It was the Crusaders in 1096 and others before that. Thus, the U.N. decision had once more robbed the villagers of the hope to which they had clung.

The first winter passed. Then on May 14, 1948, the decision was final and Israel became a state. This date was carved on the heart of every Palestinian because that was the day we became refugees in our own land. Neighboring Arab nations (Jordan, Syria, Egypt, Lebanon, and Iraq) refused to accept Israel's statehood, and within hours of the statehood decision, these nations sent forces in, trying to drive out the Jews. They all had their own agenda of power which did not consider the Palestinian people or the village of Biram. Fighting continued until the cease fire of January 1949. The Arab armies were defeated and the Jews gained more Palestinian land.

Although Palestine was predominantly a Christian nation in the early centuries, by 1944 Christians were a minority with 135,547 Christians; 553,600 Jews; and 1,061,277 Muslims. Christians were fleeing to safety in other nations as Jewish settlers were moving in. At the same time, the Muslim population was growing.

3

FAMILY DIVIDED, THEN UNITED

Father continued to pray for the soldiers as the days wore on. Families struggled to survive by working the small gardens in Gish and eating animals from the abandoned flocks.

One sultry, hot morning in the summer of 1948 we heard the ominous sound of army vehicles. I ran home to safety, not knowing what to expect. At the edge of the village the trucks stopped. A harsh voice came over a loudspeaker telling all men, young and old, to come out of their houses with hands on their heads. Fear shot through me as I watched my peaceful father and three older brothers—Rudah, Chacour and Musah—walk out to the street. Uncles and cousins came from doorways all around us.

"Turn over your guns, you Palestinian terrorists," the commander demanded. Guns? There were no guns in our village.

Through the long hot day the soldiers shouted and the mukhtars and other village men stood silently. Some men fainted from the heat. How could they produce guns they did not have? I glanced at Father and saw his lips moving in silent prayer—praying again for the soldiers.

Finally, at sundown, the loudspeaker blasted again. "Return

to your homes, but don't try to escape." Mother and Wadi rushed to bring Father and my brothers into the coolness of the house. Mother brought them water and food, and our family huddled together—safe for now, but for how long?

Weariness etched Father's face as he gently touched each family member. We each received that touch and unspoken blessing, hoping that our fears were foolish and the soldiers would leave. Father knew better.

Before long, that dreaded sound was heard again from outside as the men were once more herded out to the streets. This time they were forced, at gun-point, into the backs of open trucks. As they were driven away the loudspeaker blared: "We are taking your terrorists away. This is the punishment for all terrorists. They will not return."

The village was silent except for the sound of weeping women and children who were left behind to wonder about the fate of their husbands, fathers and sons, and to pray for their safety. Prayer became the glue that held our family together. Mother's strength was needed to reassure Wadi, Atallah and me, and also to counsel and support the other village women.

Mother prayed us through those long, lonely days. She carried on Father's tradition of evening prayer and could also be heard praying throughout the day. She prayed to Jesus like a friend, asking Him to bring peace to the land and to bring her husband Michael and the boys home safely.

I too prayed and found comfort walking alone through the silent hills. I could picture Jesus walking beside me and felt new meaning in His words, the Beatitudes, that Mother often spoke: "Blessed are those who mourn, for they will be comforted."

For three months there was no word of Father and the other men. Our prayers continued as we walked through our daily routines of school and household chores. Each night after prayers, when Wadi, Atallah and I were tucked into bed, we heard the metal door-bolt click, providing as much safety as possible for the night ahead.

One night as I drifted off to sleep, I heard a new sound.

Someone was trying to open the door. The rattling of the door-bolt quickly awakened me. Listening fearfully, I heard a voice whisper, "Let us in. Please open the door."

Mother cautiously went to the door. "Who is there?"

"Quickly, let us in. It is Michael."

Mother shrieked, "Michael," and hesitantly opened the door. On seeing Father and my brothers, she threw the door open wider. They rushed inside, closing it quickly behind them. Everyone was weeping and hugging as we experienced the answer to our prayers.

Mother brought out food and water, and we listened to Father tell their story. The night they were taken from Gish they huddled for hours in the back of the truck, bumping along the rough road. Dawn's light showed they had traveled south toward Jerusalem. As they approached the border between Jordan and the new State of Israel, the trucks stopped and the men were pushed out. They scattered as the soldiers began firing over their heads. The soldiers were driving them across the border, far away from Gish and Biram, their beloved village.

Father and my brothers managed to stay together as they fled, putting the soldiers and their gun-fire far behind them. Father hoped to find a friendly Arab village in Jordan or Syria where they might have shelter and a bit of food. What a shock it was to be turned away from village after village with the words *dirty Palestinian* ringing in their ears. As the days passed, their hunger increased.

They knew their only hope was to make their way back to Gish, and they did just that. Hunger and fear drove them on. They even groveled in the dirt for insects to keep from starving. At times, they lost their bearings but then would see something familiar. When Father spotted Mount Meron in Northern Israel, they knew they were nearly home.

They entered the village at night, in case there were soldiers standing guard. Their months of hardship seemed to fall away as they were welcomed into the shelter of our family again.

That night Father's prayer spoke of thanksgiving for a safe

return. "Lord, we give you thanks for protecting us and leading us home. As you saved our father Ishmael, Abraham's son, so too you have saved us. We claim Ishmael's blessing and pray that justice will be done in this holy land." I drifted off to sleep with Father's prayer cradled in my heart and Mother's necklace jingling merrily in my dreams. We could face anything now that we were together again.

4

INTRODUCTION *to* SETTLEMENTS

As the months wore on, a few more men returned to their homes. Some, however, were never heard from again. We lived with the uncertainty that the soldiers might return any day. They never did.

In 1950, word came of experimental communities being started. They had actually been going for many years. These agricultural communities, called kibbutzim, needed help to work the fields. It soon became clear why our men were allowed to stay home. They were hired, for low pay, to run their own farms as well as help out on the kibbutz.

Then we learned that a kibbutz was being started around our beloved village of Biram. Settlers from Europe and America would be living across the fields from the homes we had been forced to abandon. Our homes still stood empty. Our fig orchard, that Father had tended so lovingly, had been sold by the government to one of these settlers as an investment.

Oh, the pain we felt as we watched Father close his eyes in prayer. The anger we experienced at such injustice was quieted as Father told us that we must not curse those who wish us harm but ask Our Lord to bless these enemies of our people. Then we would feel God's peace within and would be able to do His will.

As I walked alone through the hills, trying to understand

what was happening, I cried out to God, "How can Father accept this cruel turn of events—all without cursing those who have wronged him? Why must his life's work, his orchards, be taken from him and given to others?"

Father's influence in the community was felt when the mukhtars worked together and drew up a petition that welcomed the settlers to the new village of Biram. The petition said we were gladly giving them this new village in hopes that they would allow us to return to our homes in the old village of Biram. In peace we could live side by side. No answer was given by the government, but our fear of the soldiers forced us to remain in Gish.

Father's next surprising move came when he applied to the new government for the job of caring for his own orchard. He was hired. Mother asked him why he would do such a thing. His reply was, "At least I will be able to care for the orchard and my beloved trees." My brothers were also given work.

Some of the young men from the village decided they would not be hired out to work on their own land. They chose to take their families and move to Haifa or Akko, in hopes of finding factory jobs in these cities along the Mediterranean Sea. They had only hostile feelings toward the new State of Israel.

Once more, the boys of our village chose soccer as a way to pass the time. At eleven, I was a better runner than a kicker, but Atallah and his friend Asad made sure I was part of the team. We stopped mid-play one afternoon when we heard cars roaring into the village.

Most of the boys, sensing trouble, ran for home. I was not so fortunate. Several jeeps and dark automobiles screeched to a stop by the sand lot and out jumped about a dozen men. I froze, unable to move. I was grabbed by the arm and so were two others .

"Where did you put the wire?" yelled the man. "Who told you to do it?" My arm ached under his strong grip.

I fought back tears. "What wire? We've been playing soccer and don't know about any wire."

"Lies!" The man screamed. "You cannot get away with terrorist actions." For what seemed like ages, the three of us were held. Then the men grabbed sticks and began beating us on the shoulders and head. As they shouted and swung their sticks, our families, who had been warned by the fleeing soccer team, gathered silently. The men began to shout at them. "What do you teach your children? How dare they cut telephone wires that lead to the kibbutz."

Father stepped forward to protect me and their fury was turned on him. "Tomorrow we will be back and you had better have the wire." Father suffered their words in silence. Then they jumped into their cars and sped off.

True to their promise, they were back in the morning, forcing Father and me to return to the police station with them. I was terrified that I would never see Mother again. Into my terror a still small voice spoke, "Peace, be still." Then I remembered the words of the Beatitudes: "Blessed are you when people falsely say all kinds of evil against you...for in the same way they persecuted the prophets before you."

As it turned out, we were questioned for many hours, and when we could give no answers, they angrily drove us back to Gish. In time the bruises from my beating healed. Many months later we learned that a wagon driver had run over the telephone wire with metal-rimmed wheels, slicing off a large section. Since he was in a hurry, he loaded the length of wire into his wagon and returned it to the kibbutz weeks later on his return trip. An apology from the police was in order but it never came.

What did come was a letter from the Supreme Court in Jerusalem. What we had hoped for had finally arrived: papers that would give us permission to return to Biram. This wonderful news erased the telephone wire incident from our minds for a while. The mukhtars joyfully took the letter to the Zionist commanding officer.

How shocked we were when he refused to honor the order. "The village is ours. This letter doesn't mean a thing. You have no right here."

How could we go on? The hurt and pain in Father's eyes were unbearable. I saw only two choices: accept the abuse of this situation or resort to violence. Again I headed for the hills and a chance to talk to My Champion, Jesus.

5

BETRAYED AGAIN

A visit from the Bishop, our church leader, provided another choice for our family. The Bishop had come to discuss ways for the villagers to deal with a new government that refused to honor the rights of Palestinians. Father also had a plan in mind and he spoke to the Bishop about it. He saw in me, his youngest son, the possibility for an education which could someday bring hope to a seemingly hopeless situation. Father had noted my hours spent alone in the Galilean hills and asked me why I did this. When I told him it was to think and pray, he began to see a need for me to leave Gish and go to school beyond our small village. Here at home, opportunities were far too limited.

And so it was that at the age of twelve I was taken to Haifa, about 75 km away. Father, Mother and I rode the bus to the orphanage where I would live while attending school. A sense of panic nearly overpowered my feelings of joy. Now, at last, I would have a chance to study the Bible and church teachings, along with the usual school subjects, but when would I see my family again?

School life was difficult. I did not really fit in as I wasn't an orphan like the others. My parents were alive and well but very far away. In my loneliness I began writing letters to Jesus, pouring out my homesickness and frustration. Studying the Bible like a history book did not satisfy my spiritual needs. My letters to Jesus took care of that.

Then one morning in January 1952 my brother Rudah appeared at the early morning church service. Perhaps he brought news of home. That he did, but it was bad news. Once more my heart seemed ready to break.

He told how the village elders had received word from the government that the people of Biram would be allowed to return home. This wonderful homecoming was set for Christmas, December 25th. With joy and excitement, preparations were made to leave Gish. Festive meals were shared. There were celebrations long into the night as Christmas carols drifted out into the darkness.

The great day dawned and the villagers joyfully walked over the hills to Biram. They arrived, only to find the village encircled by tanks, bulldozers and other military vehicles. As they watched in horror, a signal was given and the cannons opened fire, not toward the people, but toward our homes that had stood empty for so long. The homes were blown apart quickly and so was the church. Nothing was left of Biram but rubble. Rudah trembled as he told me.

"How are Mother and Father," I asked tearfully. I was not surprised when he said that Father prayed daily that God would forgive the Zionists who were responsible for our loss. He also continued to care for the orchard with the help of my brothers. His beloved trees had miraculously escaped destruction. Mother continued to serve her family, praying her way through this tremendous loss.

That night I poured my heart out in a letter to Jesus. I desperately wanted to return home to the comfort of my family, but God had other plans for me.

As I began my second year at the Bishop's school, a new boy enrolled. Faraj and I became close friends. God had provided someone to ease my loneliness. Faraj and I studied together and shared most of our waking hours. We talked about going on to a new school that was opening in Nazareth. It was for boys who wanted to serve God and the Melkite Church.

The Bishop had seen in Faraj and me a need to go beyond the classes that were offered in Haifa. He called us in separately, to see if we would like to go to the new minor seminary in Nazareth. I needed time to think and also to talk over the idea with Father and Mother. The Bishop arranged for me to go to Gish so that a decision could be made.

The joy of being home again was overshadowed by news of my grandparents' death. Both of them had died in the past year. Father looked old as he told of the destruction of Biram and admitted that he no longer was able to tend the orchard. The memories were too painful.

Our discussion on school ended with Father asking, "And what do you want to do?" This time it was my decision. I told him I wanted to go on to Nazareth. What a joy it was to bring this word to the Bishop and to learn that Faraj had made the same decision.

In 1954, Faraj and I began our studies at St. Joseph's Minor Seminary in Nazareth. Here our days of study were surrounded by serious young men and strict rules and yet an ever present feeling of God's peace. At times, my sharp tongue got me in trouble when I spoke out against something I felt was wrong or unknowingly broke a rule.

Forgetting the rule about staying in our rooms after lights out, I began to slip over to the chapel on nights that I couldn't sleep. This gave me a chance to pray and talk to My Champion, Jesus. One night, I stayed too long and fell asleep. I was awakened by a rough hand shaking me. The next day I was brought before the principal, and because of my refusal to follow the rules, was sentenced to forty days of restriction.

Father Ghazal was one of the strictest teachers at St. Joseph's, and yet the one I liked the most. One day a student asked him how a Christian should respond when others tormented or hurt him. Father Ghazal's answer struck a chord deep within me. "It is not enough to try to be good—some sort of 'saint.' You need to let God occupy your body so He can tame you. You may be put through many hard times, but He will use these struggles to train you."

Those words shaped my next decision and my life. Both Faraj and I sensed a need to continue our education even beyond St. Joseph's. The Bishop tried to open the door for us to attend a very old Melkite school in Jerusalem. This was not possible, however, because that part of the city had been given to Jordan. Now *dirty Palestinians* were not allowed. This ancient city of Jerusalem, which dates back to nearly 1000 B.C., is where three major religions—Judaism, Islam and Christianity— had their beginnings. Since the present war began in 1948, the city of Jerusalem had been divided, with the eastern portion belonging to the country of Jordan.

Just when that door to the seminary was closed, God swung another door open. The Seminary of Saint Sulpice in Paris agreed to take two eighteen-year-old Palestinian students, and so once more goodbyes were tearfully spoken as Faraj and I boarded a ship and sailed from the port city of Haifa to Paris, France, making stops at Naples and Rome, Italy.

During our four years at St. Joseph's, the Palestinian situation did not improve. Problems arose over the Gaza Strip and the Sinai Peninsula which have always been areas of importance. Gaza is a strategic port on the Mediterranean Sea, and the Sinai Peninsula separates Africa from Asia and has the Suez Canal as its eastern border. In 1955, Gaza was invaded by the Zionist forces, and the next year the Sinai Peninsula was taken. At this point, the United States stepped in and forced the Zionists to return the Sinai Peninsula to Egypt. For now, our families were safe but that was not true for all Palestinians. My heart ached for those whose lives and homes had been shattered by war and whose land had been taken for yet another kibbutz.

6

EUROPEAN EDUCATION

Our first challenge at St. Sulpice was to learn French. This we did, along with our other studies. As we learned the language, we began to realize there was another problem—students at St. Sulpice were curious to learn about the "Holy Land." This name was given to Israel because it is holy to Christians, Jews and Muslims (people who practice Islam). But as soon as we mentioned the sufferings of our people, the Palestinians, the conversation ended. The sympathy of the world had been turned toward the Jews because of their tremendous suffering during the Holocaust. No one wanted to hear that the "homeland" of Israel, where the Jews had gone for safety, already belonged to the Palestinians. It seemed that everyone believed the newspapers' view of Palestinians: that we were all terrorists. Our fellow students were willing to admit that there might be a few good Palestinians, like Faraj and me, but there were not many. How deeply this hurt us.

Our homesickness during the Christmas holiday was recognized by members of the church. One of the wealthier families invited me to spend Christmas with them and some family friends. Faraj was invited to visit another family. My host said he would introduce me as his "special guest" and he did just that. What a shock it was to hear him explain that I was a Jewish student from Bethlehem who was studying at the seminary.

I tried to correct him but he quickly moved the conversation forward. I was so upset and embarrassed that I said very little that evening and was happy to return to the lonely dormitory. Then I understood that the invitation was not given out of kindness but to provide his guests with a *special attraction*, a Jew from Bethlehem. Being a Palestinian was like having leprosy.

Our studies at St. Sulpice became more frustrating to me as time went on. We seemed to be learning about God as though we were looking at the Bible's teaching through a microscope. Little was said about prayer and letting God's Spirit dwell in our hearts. When I talked to Faraj about my feelings, he said we must not question our teachers but must learn to serve the church quietly. With those words I realized that a split was developing between us. Our service to God would take different paths. I didn't know then that my path would often lead over dangerous ground.

Faraj and I still shared our thoughts but we disagreed more often than before. We both felt a spiritual emptiness in the European people we met through the church, however. They seemed far more concerned with material things and comfortable living than they were about deepening their relationship with God. As Faraj put it: "The real problem with their belief is that they think man is the center of all things and they try to fit God in where it feels comfortable. We believe God is the center of all things and we must learn how we fit into His plan."

My reply came from the heart. "With these strange ideas, no wonder people say God is *dead*. They *killed* Him! They give Him no value or respect, and, without God, people don't care about each other either." How I wished I could talk to my professors about these concerns. I tried, but was sharply told that my ideas were not acceptable.

This was a troubled time for us to be in Europe—the 1960s. World leaders called it *The Cold War*—a time when there were no major wars in the world but some of the larger nations of the world treated each other as enemies. The coldness was really fear. Nations were afraid of other nations. There was no trust. People who spoke or worked for peace were often killed for their trouble. Ever since the atomic bomb was dropped on Japan on August 6, 1945, world leaders knew that nuclear weapons could destroy the world. In Israel, the Zionists were also spreading fear. As the tension and fear built, small groups of Palestinians called *fedayeen* banded together to fight back.

In 1962, I got word that my brother Chacour was dead. He had been living in Haifa with his wife and eight small children. His job was in construction so the work was hard and heavy. He had suffered a stroke. He lived about forty days after that before his heart finally gave out. With this news, a deep sadness filled my heart. I wanted so badly to go home to Israel to be with Chacour's family and give them my support. Since I had very little money, a long trip like that was impossible. The school did give me some time off, however, to go to a quiet Christian retreat center to work through my sorrow.

As I rode alone on the train, I was jolted back to dark reality by a small blonde child who wanted to be my friend. He climbed up on my lap and soon we were laughing and playing together. His parents, Franz and Lony Gruber, came looking for him and we began chatting like old friends. By the time we got off the train, we seemed like family, and they had invited me to visit them in West Germany. This I would do many times in future years.

Reality hit with a thud as we stood on the platform, having our passports carefully checked by dark-suited officials. My imagination caused me to jump back in history to 1937. I saw those men as helmeted Nazi soldiers of the Third Reich. Sweat broke out on my forehead as I realized that if this were 1937, my Israeli passport would have given me a ticket to the gas chambers with no questions asked. No one would have believed that I was an Arab Palestinian rather than a Jew. At that instant I had an overwhelming compassion for the Jews of Germany who had lost their lives or their families during the Holocaust in World War II. The Holocaust was that time in history when over six million Jews were killed by the military power of the

Third Reich under the leadership of Hitler.

As my thoughts jumped back to the present, I wondered why the Jews, who had been so devastated by the Holocaust, were now turning their tragic history into a tragedy for the Palestinians. The Zionists of Israel were saying that Palestinians were worthless people, always thinking about violence. The voices of hate were now shouting *Palestinian terrorist* or *dirty Palestinian*. Just as the world and church leaders said nothing to stop the Holocaust, now they were saying nothing about the persecution of my people, the Palestinians.

This haunting step back into history drove me to the libraries of Paris as soon as I returned to school. Perhaps, if I learned more about the history of the Jews, I would better understand this Jewish tragedy that seemed to be causing the spread of Zionism in my native land.

7

DISCOVERING MY PEOPLE
through ZIONIST EYES

I was shocked by what I read. According to Zionist teaching, the land of Palestine was chosen because it was *uninhabited*, and then they had turned this *wasteland* into a paradise by irrigating and planting thousands of acres. The Zionist movement had been started in Basle, Switzerland, in 1897, by a well-known writer, Theodor Herzl. His plan was drawn up at the First Zionist Congress and was designed to move European Jews, who were living in big city slums, to this *empty* land, called Palestine. Many people did not agree with his view that "Palestine was a land without a people, waiting for a people without a land," but their voices were not heard.

The more I read, the more furious I became. No mention had been made of my people, the Palestinians, whose ancestors had lived in this land since before the time of Abraham, nearly 4000 years ago. People soon forgot that Herzl had also considered setting up a Jewish *homeland* in Argentina or Uganda. The Zionists, who were not necessarily religious Jews, felt that Zionism was their Messiah, or Savior. Orthodox Jews, those who applied ancient law codes to their behavior, felt that Zionism was a blasphemy, or act of not showing reverence to God.

We Palestinians had suffered for hundreds of years under the rule of the Turkish Ottoman Empire. This empire was already falling apart in the early 1900s when World War I (1914-1918) swept across Europe and the Middle East (southeast Asia and northern Africa). My people struggled through daily life, praying that someday their cruel Turkish rulers would be overthrown.

After the war, we began to feel the breath of freedom as the League of Nations was started in 1922. The League was made up of large, powerful nations who joined together to help weaker nations, like Palestine, set up independent governments. Under this Mandate System the British were able to push the Turks out of Palestine. Then the British were given the power to set up a temporary government in Palestine, with the idea that they would leave as soon as Palestinians could manage their own government.

The next years were full of secret meetings between the British, the French, and the Russians, as they set up a government that was run by international leaders, not Palestinians. Then, a group of Christians in Britain, called Restorationists, began to say that the Second Coming of Christ was near because of the establishment of Israel as the Jewish *homeland*. Many people listened and hoped that what they said was true.

The Zionist movement swept on and grew as groups of homeless Jews from Europe were quietly starting kibbutzim throughout the land of Palestine. The population of this land in 1917 had been 92% Palestinian Arab and 8% Jew. Among the Palestinian Arabs about 51% were Christian and 49% were Muslim. By 1947, due to the immigration of European Jews, there were 67% Arab Palestinians (both Muslims and Christians) and 33% Jews. Many of my people had left their homeland for safety in other parts of the world. We now could be counted among the world's refugees, who had to flee our country to escape danger.

I read on. Deep sadness filled my spirit as I read about the wars that had engulfed the Middle East in 1948 and 1956. I could not understand the twisted logic of the Zionists who were responsible for the bombing of the King David Hotel in Jerusalem, where nearly 100 people were killed. This horrible act was then blamed on Palestinians, hoping to prove the unfounded claim that Palestinians were terrorists. How shocked I was to learn that David Ben Gurion, who was later to become Israeli Prime Minister, was well aware of this plot, as were others who were either unable or unwilling to change things.

I read about how the Haganah, a strong Zionist underground, had smuggled arms into Iraq. On several occasions Jewish communities in Iraq were the targets of bomb blasts. This too was with the knowledge of Ben Gurion and the claim was that a fanatic Arab group was responsible. The hope of the Haganah, in these terrorist acts, was to frighten the Jews in Iraq badly enough that they would flee to Israel and join in the ever growing group of settlers in the kibbutzim.

I prayed to Jesus, My Champion, that I might be able to understand these terrible events and, with His help, to rise above the anger that filled my spirit. Into my anguish came His answer. The enemy of my people and of peace was not Zionism but the demon of Militarism whose motto seemed to be, "Might makes right. Achieve your own ends by whatever means necessary—all in the name of God."

With this knowledge, I stopped my search for truth and turned instead toward the task of finishing up my seminary education at St. Sulpice and making plans for my future. Now, more that ever, I wanted to be part of God's plan to bring peace to His *holy land* and to all of Abraham's children—both Arab and Jew.

I felt I was called to be the salt that Jesus spoke of in Matthew—salt that would sting in the open wound of hatred that was festering in my homeland—not salt that had lost its savor. My role would be an active one. My charge was different from God's call for Faraj and for my father. For them, being a Christian was to patiently bear whatever came your way. However, all three of us prayerfully followed wherever and however God led us.

8

Airport Patience—
Then Ordination

Faraj and I completed our studies at St. Sulpice and began to make plans for our return home to Palestine. Before leaving Europe, I wanted to make one more trip to Germany to visit Lony, Franz and Wolfgang. I had received an invitation to visit and this time they seemed more insistent than usual.

When I arrived, I understood why. They had gotten me a going away present that they knew I would need. It was a white Volkswagen. I was overwhelmed by their kindness and generosity. None of us knew then the important part that little car would have in my life.

Faraj had made other travel plans and we agreed to meet in Nazareth for our ordination. I accompanied my car on a ship going from Genoa, Italy, to Haifa, Israel. It was with mixed feelings that I was leaving Europe. I was excited about returning home to my family but knew the safety and security I had felt in Europe were not available to Palestinians in the land now called Israel.

I prayed for wisdom and strength to deal with whatever came my way as I hurried toward the customs area after the ship had docked. With passport in hand I could see my eager family straining to catch a glimpse of me as I proceeded through the line. The customs official glanced at my passport, ready to stamp it for entry. Then he said, "Oh, you're Palestinian. You'll have to step into that room over there."

Once inside the room, I was questioned for half an hour about my reasons for being in Paris, whom I had stayed with, where I had traveled, who my contacts were. The tension was building as I patiently answered these questions, wondering if I would ever get out of this room. Finally, he got to his feet and I followed, thinking I would now be on my way with my passport correctly stamped.

Instead, he said, "Strip!"

"Excuse me?"

"You must be completely searched. Take off all your clothes." By now he was red in the face from anger.

I could not do what he asked even though I knew he had the power to refuse to let me enter my own country. I sat down abruptly and began rummaging in my suitcase.

"What do you think you're doing?" he shouted.

"Getting a book to read. I'm not going to strip and you're not going to let me out of this room. I might as well read this book I just bought."

He was furious, and for eight tense hours I sat and read. At his wits' end, he suddenly shoved my stamped passport into my hand and pointed to the door. Although I was shaking inside, I carefully put my book back in my bag and headed for the door and the open arms of my welcoming family.

And so, in 1965, I reentered my world: the uneasy world of the Palestinian, who may be stopped and questioned any time, any place, for no apparent reason.

I tried to forget my unpleasant welcome as plans swept along toward ordination: that official church ceremony for which I had studied and prayed during those many, long years. The Bishop had come to St. Joseph's Church in Nazareth for my ordination and that of Faraj. The church was filled with family and friends, eagerly waiting to hear the words that would officially invest us with priestly authority. Then came the laying on of hands and the prayer that God's Spirit would flow into us. Next, Faraj and I were each introduced to the congregation with the words, "He is Worthy."

As those words "He is Worthy" rang in my ears and echoed through my whole being, I sensed my inadequacy and knew that only God could make me worthy to be a servant in His kingdom. I accepted the challenge and was ready to move on toward God's goal for my life.

As the days passed after that great ordination ceremony, I waited to hear from the Bishop about my first assignment. In my waiting, I felt a strange restlessness stirring within me. Perhaps a trip to Biram, the village of my childhood that had been destroyed by Zionist soldiers, would settle my spirit.

And so I went. One morning, just before dawn, I started out in my little white Volkswagen. I bumped over the rough roads, wondering what I would find. The sun came up and the beauty of those rolling hills shone in the light of a new day. I parked the car and began to walk toward home, my first home. It was a pile of rubble now—twisted doorposts, crumbling walls. Startled birds flitted away at my step.

I stood amid the ruins of our little church, head bowed, unable to go on. Memories flooded into my heart as I seemed to hear the laughter of children and the praying voices of the elders. Into my brokenness God's voice whispered, "He is worthy."

I vowed that one day, with God's help, I would return to Biram and rebuild what was broken. There would be a new beginning for my people. Before I left, I headed for Father's orchard. Those beloved fig trees still stood in the rocky soil. My special tree, the one I loved to climb, was there and so was the one to which Father had grafted six different varieties of fig. Now, each different branch was a sturdy part of the fig tree. Each branch was getting nourishment from the same roots, embedded in the same soil. All were of equal importance.

So too were the many families in God's kingdom. As it says in the book of Galatians: "There is neither Jew nor Greek, slave

nor free, male nor female but all are equal in God's sight."
There is neither Arab nor Jew, but all are descendants of
Abraham and equal in God's eyes. Jews and Arab Palestinians,
working together, could rebuild what has been broken.

As I turned to go, my eyes fell on a sign written in English
and Hebrew. It said that these *antiquities were preserved and protected*
by the government. Then I remembered the news that tourists
now came on buses to view the ruins of my beloved Biram. I
walked slowly back to the car, knowing that God had led me to
this place to help me realize the vastness of His plan for my
life. With that knowledge came the assurance that My Champion, Jesus, would be with me every step of the way.

9

STRANGE WELCOME *in* IBILLIN

I bumped along the rutted roads in my little VW. As I went, I puzzled over the Bishop's words as he had explained my first assignment a few days earlier. I had never heard of this place called Ibillin, a village of several thousand people. It was about a thirty minute drive from Nazareth, in upper Galilee.

Ibillin, with Haifa in the background

What did the Bishop mean when he said it was a poor village and would not be an easy assignment? He said, "Try it for a month; no harm in that." If things didn't work out, he assured me of a new assignment. The church had not had the services of a priest for some time and had been left in the charge of a church member he referred to as the Responsible. A letter had been sent to the Responsible to tell him of my coming.

After losing my way several times, I finally arrived in Ibillin and found my way to the church. Excitement welled within me as I stepped out of the car for my first view of the place where my life's work would begin.

To my dismay, the church was badly in need of repair. The door was hanging sadly on a broken, rusting hinge. I stared in disbelief. Then I heard an angry voice behind me. "Get out of here. Turn your car around and get out!" There stood a furious middle-aged man, eyes bright with rage. Was this the chairman of the *Welcoming Committee*?

"I'm Elias Chacour, the new priest."

"I know exactly who you are. I received the Bishop's letter saying you would come today."

That was my introduction to the Responsible. My first thought was to jump in the car and drive back to the Bishop's office in Nazareth to ask for a new assignment. Suddenly, the words from my ordination ceremony came to mind: "He is worthy." I knew then that I would not leave. Instead, I took a deep breath, grabbed the hand of the angry Responsible and said, "Let's pray together."

He seemed to relax a bit as I prayed. "God, draw us together as Christian brothers. Help us work out our differences."

Still angry, the Responsible began a long list of reasons why I should not stay. First of all, he demanded that I return all the things that had been stolen by the former priest. I could not believe my eyes or my ears as he dragged me by the arm into the dimly lit church. The broken down door had let in rain and scorching sun, so the paint was peeling and faded. There were a few warped wooden benches and a stone altar, but that was all.

"See," shouted the Responsible. "The last priest disappeared one night with all of our furnishings: the cup and plate used for Communion, most of the benches and even the outdoor toilet."

Then he pulled me outside into the courtyard and pointed to the dilapidated building next to the church. "That's the parish house. If you stay, that's where you'll live." His voice was not as harsh as he showed me the two small rooms inside. What a sight! There was a greasy stove and a battered kerosene lamp which stood at the edge of a rickety three-legged table. There was no bed, and the outdoor toilet had gone off with the last priest. The only water came from a leaky outdoor spigot. So this was the Bishop's *challenge*. One month was all he asked, and with God's help, I could do that.

In the strongest voice I could manage, I announced, "I'll be staying. This is fine." The Responsible watched me as I hauled my suitcase in from the car. Then he turned abruptly and left.

I pondered my next move as I dragged a few benches from the church over to the parish house. Somehow, these would have to do for a bed. I unpacked and tried to make those shabby rooms look like home. I wasn't too successful.

I knew in my heart that a church was more than a building, however decayed, and more than a priest, however hopeful. I set out for the streets of Ibillin in search of my congregation: the people to fill the church and sing praises to God.

I was in for another shock. The village of Ibillin was decaying as badly as the church. The village dated back to at least 325 A.D., when one of the church fathers had played an important role in the Council of Nicea, a famous church conference. In later years, Ibillin had been a battlefield for Crusader and Islamic armies during the Crusades (late 11th to late 13th centuries). The Crusades were a series of wars that were fought by Christians against the infidels: those who were against Christian beliefs. The purpose of the Crusades was to protect the holy places in Palestine from destruction and to convert or eliminate the infidels.

In modern times, Ibillin was still struggling from the effects of war. Since 1948, many people had settled in the village when they fled from other areas. Muslims and Christians, both Melkite and Greek Orthodox, tried unsuccessfully to get along. Neighbors did not trust neighbors and each religious group tried to control the village councils. Hatred spread and with it came delinquency and alcoholism as young people tried to grow up in a hopeless environment.

There was even hatred within families. In one family of four grown brothers, the hate was so strong that if two of the men came upon each other on the street, other villagers ran for cover, afraid of the dreadful fight that might occur. One of the brothers was a village policeman and all were believers and members of the church. How sad! Where was the love of Christ here?

Into this seemingly desperate situation I stepped. The words of My Champion, Jesus, came to mind: "Blessed are the peacemakers, for they shall be called the children of God." In one month could I make a difference in this hate-filled village? With God's help, I vowed to try.

The Responsible, in his efforts to control things, had driven people from attending worship services. He felt it was up to him to decide who was worthy to attend, and not many people were good enough in his eyes. My first job was to change that. The only way I could see to do it would be by visiting every family in Ibillin, whether Christian, Jew or Muslim. It was a tremendous challenge, but very necessary, if I hoped to bring God's love into this unfriendly place.

As I visited home after home, I was welcomed, timidly at first. Hospitality is so deeply ingrained in our culture that my visits were blessed with coffee, fruit, and some of their carefully hoarded sweets. Conversation, that was reluctantly started, soon began to show promise. From time to time men would offer to do some repair work at the church or parish house or make new benches.

Although I was welcomed into village homes, very few families accepted my invitation to come back to church. I could see how unrealistic my plan was to visit each family. That would take years, not only one month. I really needed help, but who?

Then I remembered Mother Josephate, a deeply spiritual woman and a good friend, who was the leader of a community of Christian women in Nazareth. These sisters dedicated their lives to living simply and serving those in need. Perhaps she would send two sisters from her community to help me in Ibillin. I decided to go and find out.

As I told her of the need in Ibillin and my hope that two sisters would be available to come and work with the women and perhaps the children of the village, she listened patiently. "It would be a way to spread God's love," I added. She said she thought my request had come "not from me but from the heart of God." She agreed to ask her superior, the person in charge of the community. She told me to come back in several weeks for her answer, which she assured me would be yes.

While waiting for her answer, I continued my visits. The Responsible, seeing that he was losing control of me and the church, began to go along on the visits. He tried to tell me whom to see and what to say. He was visibly upset when I announced that I was planning to visit Habib, the man who lived next to the church. Habib had angered the Responsible by speaking out against his ideas and so was no longer welcome to attend church. Over the Responsible's strong protests, I climbed the steps to Habib's house "just to say hello," I thought. Two hours later, after a delightful visit, I returned to the courtyard. The furious Responsible had gone home.

My visit was not forgotten, however, by either Habib or the Responsible. Habib was so grateful for the love I had shown by my visit that he presented me with a small grapevine and a young lemon tree. Together, we planted them in the courtyard, near Habib's house. I carefully tended them and they grew beautifully.

Several weeks later, the Responsible came to tell me I had to get rid of that dreadful vine which Habib had given me. As I prayed for guidance, I asked the Responsible to bring me a bucket of water. He agreed, as he knew the vine would be easier to uproot if we dampened the soil first.

How shocked he was when I poured the water slowly over the vine tree, made the sign of the cross and said, "Oh, vine tree, I baptize you Christian in the name of the Father, the Son, and the Holy Spirit. The one who uproots you will be uprooted. The one who waters you will be watered by God's grace." The startled Responsible did not dare to say more and the vine tree was saved for a long, productive life.

As the Responsible's control of the church and its people began to crumble, my confidence began to grow. I was surprised to wake up one morning with the sudden realization that one month had long since passed and my ministry was starting to have a look of promise. The next day I would go to visit Mother Josephate and complete the arrangements to bring two sisters to work with me in Ibillin.

10

GOD'S WILL PREVAILS

The next day, as I stood before Mother Josephate, I could tell from the look on her face that all was not well. She patiently explained that her superior's answer was no. When she could not assure him that the sisters would be working with Roman Catholics, or that people would be converted, or changed to become Roman Catholics, he would not grant her request.

I was crushed. My plans for a school for Palestinian children and parenting classes for young mothers could not be carried out without the help of the sisters. As I turned to go, she spoke again.

"You know the difficult position I am in. I have always supported my superior's authority because I know he has been placed over me by the Church. I also know I must answer to a higher authority—God. So I have decided to respect my superior's wishes and not send two sisters to help, but I will send three." Her eyes sparkled as she told me her decision. I was overjoyed, and we determined that I should return the next Sunday to pick up the three sisters who would help me do God's work in Ibillin.

I arrived bright and early the following Sunday and was introduced to the three nuns, or sisters. All three were dressed in identical gray clothes, or habits. Mere Macaire was tall and dignified looking, a bit older than I had hoped. Sister Ghislaine was short and rather round. She had the look of a beloved grandmother and seemed to be quite intelligent. Sister Nazarena was of medium height and very thin. I soon learned that she had a wonderful way with children.

As we were getting into the car, one of the nuns remarked, "You will bring us back to the convent right after the worship service, won't you?" I was about to say that was not possible when I caught Mother Josephate's eye. She nodded *Yes*, and I found myself assuring the nuns that they would be back in Nazareth right after the service of liturgy.

What was I to do? I needed the help of these nuns for more than just the hour of worship. They had their own ideas, however, and right after the liturgy they marched out to the car and waited impatiently for me to drive them back to the convent. I was amazed when they asked me to pick them up the following Sunday. They liked going to Ibillin to pray at the little church. Each week, for six weeks, I played taxi driver for these three nuns, but no help was given for the needy people of the parish.

When I asked Mother Josephate how long this could go on, she explained that the nuns had a *convent mentality*. They were used to getting up at a certain time, eating at a certain time, and doing everything according to the convent rules. It was hard for them to think for themselves. She advised me to be patient.

As always, I prayed for guidance. By the next Sunday I had a plan. Instead of rushing the nuns back to Nazareth, I made a small lunch for them and also invited some of the church women to come and meet them. I let the women know that the nuns were skilled in nursing. As soon as we got to the parish house after the liturgy, people began to come, some of them bearing gifts of food for the visiting nuns. One young mother, her face lined with worry, brought her two-year-old child, whose small body shook with chills and fever. The nuns gathered around the worried mother, and Sister Nazarena gently took the child from her arms and settled into the rocking chair. Mere Macaire and Sister Ghislaine asked the mother questions about the boy and gave her suggestions about his care. Soon, Ibrahim, the baby, was sound asleep in Sister Nazarena's arms. A special bond of love and trust seemed to enfold them as they rocked.

Our trip back to Nazareth was filled with excited chatter. It didn't seem to matter that it was well into the evening. The sisters were busy making plans to bring cold medicines, aspirin and other remedies when they came the next week. Yes, of course they would stay all day Sunday. I cautiously suggested that we could visit some of the families from the parish. All three agreed. I smiled to myself, and said a silent *Thank you, Lord*.

The love that the people of the parish shared with the nuns on Sundays somehow overflowed to me during the week as gifts of food began coming. I had been here six months now and was beginning to feel like this was home and I belonged. At least most people were happy about my ministry.

The Responsible, however, did not like what was happening. As the nuns and I were building bridges of love within the parish, he was fanning the flames of hate. The idea that a twenty-six-year-old priest was leading the congregation and he was no longer in charge of things made him very angry. He was not comfortable with the thought of my visiting all the people of the parish and inviting them to church. He reminded people of past hatreds and tried to set their minds against me. Some listened. Others liked the sense of love and caring that was beginning to develop. I knew something had to be done as the storm clouds were gathering within the parish.

Meanwhile, the Sunday visits of the nuns were accomplishing more and more. People's health needs were being cared for and church families were developing friendships. The number of people who came on Sunday for liturgy began to grow a little. Past hostilities were not forgotten, even when people worshipped together in the same building. These walls of hatred were not easily torn down. With sadness in my heart, I took these concerns to Jesus in prayer.

How surprised I was when one Sunday, as I arrived at the convent, I was met by the three nuns who were carrying suitcases. "We decided it would be easier if we lived in Ibillin, if that

is all right with you." I could have kissed them. Instead, I enthu-
siastically agreed with their decision and loaded the suitcases
into the car before they could change their minds. Mother
Josephate nodded her approval as we drove off.

As that well-loaded little Volkswagen bumped over the
roads on the way to Ibillin, I struggled with a new dilemma:
where would they stay? The facilities in the parish house had
not improved much. I was still sleeping on the hard benches I
had brought over from the church. After the morning worship
service I spoke with some of the church members about our
problem and soon was able to find three metal-framed beds. I
breathed a sigh of relief as I helped the nuns get settled. It was
soon obvious that the two-room parish house was not large
enough for all of us. My only choice seemed to be to make my
bed in the Volkswagen. It was rather cramped but I managed to
stay warm and dry. I wrote to Lony and Franz, thanking them
for my *bedroom on wheels*.

The storm clouds rolled on. The Responsible was furious
when I opened our church doors to the Muslims from a neighboring mosque. After the mosque—their place of worship—
was struck by lightning, the people could no longer go there for
prayer, at least until it was repaired. I spoke with Abu
Muhammad, the Muslim clergyman. At first he was reluctant to
pray in our church because Muslims do not pray in a Christian
church.

"Why not?" I argued. "You praise God during your prayers,
don't you? I do not pray better than you do, Abu Muhammad.
You and your people are welcome to pray in our church." That
was the beginning of a better relationship between Muslims and
Christians in Ibillin.

Late one cold winter night, a message came that one of the
old women of the church was dying. Her son, Abu Mouhib, the
hated village policeman, wanted me to come. I had never before
attended to someone who was dying. As Abu Mouhib let me in
to the dying woman's room, the dislike he had for me hovered
in the air. I took her icy hand in mine, and for hours I sat by her

side as her breathing slowly stopped. I gently closed her eyes and went to the other room to report her death.

I offered to notify the other three brothers as I left in the early morning hours. To my surprise, Abu Mouhib growled, "NO! My brothers do not set foot in my house. If they dare to come, you will have five funerals on your hands because we will kill each other."

The coldness of that intense hatred followed me home. As I crawled into the back seat of my little Volkswagen, I grieved for the loss of a mother as well as the anger that gripped her sons like a vise. Sleep would not come, and when it did, my dreams were filled with memories of the hatred I had seen on the soldiers' faces in Biram and the military policeman who shook me so badly when, as a small boy, I was accused of cutting a wire. Over all of these memories, the image of the Responsible's smug face drifted in and out of the picture.

By now, I had been in Ibillin a year and a half, and the thought of leaving was long forgotten. My regular home visits and the loving nursing care given by the nuns was greatly appreciated. And yet, attendance at church had not improved much since the beginning of my ministry. This was not true, however, during the Christmas and Easter seasons. Then the church was often full to overflowing.

I prayed daily for a way to crumble the walls of hatred that separated families and neighbors within the church. So it was that on Palm Sunday there were more than 250 people in our small church. They were packed in like sardines. We left the doors open to get air circulating and so that our songs of praise could drift outside. As I began the liturgy, I looked out on a sea of stony faces. Where was their joy?

With a lump in my throat, I led the service. Hymns and responses were sung half heartedly, and I knew in my heart that God was not pleased. At the end of the service, when the congregation stood for the benediction (the blessing that would end the service), I did the unexpected. With long strides I walked to the back of the church, took a chain I had brought from the car and concealed beneath my robe, looped it through the now closed door handles and secured it with a large padlock.

Returning to the front, I faced the people. Slowly and fearfully I began to speak. "Sitting in this building does not make you a Christian. Loving your brothers and forgiving those who have wronged you are the marks of a Christian. As you know, the door is locked. I have the key. The only way you may leave this building is by killing me and taking the key or making peace with those you hate.

"For many months I've tried to unite you. I've failed because I'm only a man. But there is someone else who can bring you together in true unity. His name is Jesus Christ. He is the one who gives you power to forgive. So now I will be quiet and allow Him to give you that power. If you will not forgive, we will stay locked in here. You can kill each other and I'll provide your funerals, free."

Then I waited. I could see the nuns in the front row, faces white and lips moving in prayer. Five, then ten minutes passed. Finally Abu Mouhib, the hated policeman rose to his feet. He stood a moment with head bowed. Then with a faltering voice he said, "I'm sorry. I'm the worst one of all. I've hated my own brothers. Hated them so much I wanted to kill them. More than any of you, I need forgiveness." Then, turning to me, "Can you forgive me, too, Abuna?"

I couldn't believe my ears. *Abuna* is a title that means *our father* and is filled with love and respect.

"Of course, I forgive you." With those words I gave him a warm embrace. "Now, go and greet your brothers."

As he walked down the aisle, his three brothers rushed to meet him. Soon all were hugging, with tears streaming down their cheeks. As I looked around the church, other long-standing enemies were speaking words of forgiveness, followed by tears and hugs. This continued for nearly an hour.

Into this joy I spoke the words to end the Palm Sunday service and suggested that we sing an Easter hymn, for surely our congregation had risen from the dead, just as our Lord had done so long ago.

The doors were flung open as families and neighbors joyfully sang God's praises, at first inside the church and then outside in the streets of Ibillin. The only quiet observer was the Responsible, who stiffly accepted my embrace, but seemed unable to share the joy. And yet I knew that day was a turning point for our little congregation. Praise the Lord!

11

COMMITTEE *of* BIRAM'S PEACE MARCH

As the walls of hatred began to crumble, doors of opportunity began to open. One of the things the young people in Ibillin lacked was an education. The Israeli government provided schooling for Palestinian children only up through eighth grade. This was not enough education for them to become anything but servants or shop keepers. With the system as it was, no Palestinian youth could hope to become a doctor, lawyer, teacher, or anything else that required education.

As I talked to the nuns about my concerns, we decided to step in and make some changes. Our beginnings were small. During their years of schooling, the young people had learned to read well, but once school days were over, there were few books available. I had acquired many books during my years of study, so we opened a library in the parish house where villagers could check out my books. The people came, young and old, eager to borrow them. The books were treated with care and returned quickly so they could check out something else.

Although I enjoyed the company of the nuns, I longed to visit more with the people of the parish. Home visits took many hours each day, and so I began inviting the people to visit me at the parish house. The room that was used for a library had a small desk where I could study and write sermons. I told the people whenever my light was on or the door was open they were welcome to pay me a visit. They were delighted and often I had many visitors in one day.

Since my great concern was for the children, I prayed for a way to reach out to them. I remembered those wonderful hours that I had sat with my sister and brothers, listening to Mother tell stories from the Bible. So, Sunday afternoons were set aside for story time for the children. What a joy it was for me to help these little ones learn to love My Champion, Jesus. They learned to love Him as a friend, as I had done as a young boy. Old Testament stories also came alive as we took trips out into the hills of Galilee to walk where the prophets, as well as Jesus and his disciples, had walked long ago.

Before long, the many children who came to listen and learn were not able to fit in that small room. It was then that the idea of a community center was born. As I talked about this with the nuns, they told of another need that they had seen. "The small children need a kindergarten to keep them off the streets until they are old enough for school. They would be able to learn singing, drawing, Bible stories, games, numbers, and letters." This had also been my dream that was born long before my visit to Mother Josephate.

Before a community center could be built, we decided to enlarge the parish house. The nuns still had the two rooms on the ground floor, and so it was determined that we would build three rooms upstairs: one would be my bedroom and the other was to be used for the library and meetings, social events, programs, plays and a club for the elderly. The construction work was done by men in the parish. The library was rapidly growing as families brought in books from their homes to share, and money was donated to buy additional books.

During these busy years, Bishop Hakim invited me to study for a master's degree at Hebrew University in Jerusalem. At first, I said that was impossible. After he explained how important it was for me to understand the faith of my Jewish brothers

and sisters, I finally agreed. That three-hour drive from Ibillin
to Jerusalem and back became very tiring and meant time away
from my ministry. I was greatly blessed, however, by the opportunity to learn more about the Jewish Bible and theology. I
graduated at the end of two years and became the first Palestinian as well as the first Christian priest to earn a degree at Hebrew University. My degree was in Bible and in Talmud, the
important writings of Jewish traditions. While at the university,
I met many people from other countries who were also studying there. These contacts proved to be valuable in the years
ahead.

A new bishop had been elected to lead the Melkite churches
in all of Galilee. Bishop Joseph Raya was from Lebanon but had
a keen interest in the problems of Palestinians. He knew much
about the ways of non-violence, as he had lived in the United
States during the 1950s and 1960s and had marched in the
Civil Rights Movement with Martin Luther King, Jr. He had
heard about my village of Biram, that had been destroyed by the
Zionist soldiers. He spoke to me about finding a way to help
the villagers return home.

Golda Meir was Prime Minister of Israel at that time, and
Bishop Raya suggested that we should visit her and see if she
would help us get our confiscated village of Biram back, as well
as the neighboring village of Ikrit. It was the summer of 1972
when we were ushered into her office. She was not happy to see
us. After we told our story and made our request, she looked at
us coldly and said, "Impossible. For state reasons we cannot allow you to return." Nothing would change her mind. At another
time, when someone asked her what she planned to do about
the Palestinian issue, her reply was, "What is a Palestinian? Such
a thing does not exist."

Bishop Raya's response was to declare a day of mourning
for the thirty-three Melkite churches in Galilee. All the
churches were closed the following Sunday, and the church bells
loudly rang to announce the death of justice in Israel.

Although many people heard of our actions in response to

the Prime Minister's decision, Bishop Raya felt that more needed to be done. The Committee of Biram was formed and a protest march was planned. It was set for August 23, 1972. There was much publicity about the march, and I was asked to lead it, since Biram had been my home. We spent many months organizing this march. At first, I was afraid that no one would want to risk their lives to participate. To my surprise, on that great day there were thousands of marchers who gathered at the Jaffa Gate in the Old City of Jerusalem. There were people from all faiths: Jews, Christians, Muslims, and Druze (a combination of all three faiths). There were even about seventy professors from Hebrew University who joined the march.

This march was dangerous for all of us. We were met along the way by Israeli police and soldiers, all with weapons ready. Our objective was to meet again with Golda Meir. We gathered in front of her office, but no second interview was granted. Instead, we were interviewed by many journalists, and news of our non-violent protest march was covered in newspapers all over the world. At last, the world knew of the sad story of Biram and Ikrit.

Bishop Raya, because of his support of the protest march, was no longer thought of as a friend of the Israeli government. In the past, the Melkite church fathers had tried to live peacefully under the Israeli government, never speaking out against the injustices to Palestinians. Bishop Raya believed that it was the job of God's church to speak out against injustice. In less than two years, my dear friend Bishop Raya was transferred elsewhere, and a new man, who was not likely to cause trouble, took his place.

God's spirit continued to move through the homes and streets of Ibillin. There was a sense of hope as neighbors of different religions began to respect each other and work together on projects that would benefit them all. The nuns continued to accept all children into the kindergarten, and village programs and meetings were open to all. I was accepted as a messenger of God sent to spread love and hope among His people and welcomed into the homes of all faiths.

Unfortunately, after six years of hard work in Ibillin, our dear Mere Macaire died. Her advanced age and the harsh living conditions in Ibillin had taken their toll. She was greatly missed by everyone in the village.

The work of Sister Ghislaine and Sister Nazarena continued to expand. Word of the wonderful things they had done spread to neighboring villages, and before long I was receiving letters from priests in other churches, asking me to locate more nuns who would be willing to leave the comfort and security of the convent to help them set up kindergartens and libraries. Mother Josephate was very helpful and was able to recruit twenty-one young nuns to go out to the parishes of Galilee and spread God's love through the use of their teaching and nursing skills.

During one of my last visits with Bishop Raya, before his transfer, I was sharing my frustration with him about the lack of good schools and teaching materials. He suggested that, instead of complaining about the situation, I should do something to solve the problem.

As I drove back to Ibillin, I fumed over his words. Wasn't I already overworked enough. How could I be expected to build schools and locate up-to-date teaching materials. Into my anger and frustration came the words from St. Paul's letter to the Philippians, Chapter 4, Verse 13: "I can do all things through Christ who strengthens me." I knew in that moment that God would lead the way, once more, to accomplish the impossible. And, as always, He was true to His word.

12

BIRAM'S TREES
for PEACE REJECTED

I loved working with the children. Their enthusiasm was contagious. The Committee of Biram decided to involve the youth in their celebration of Israel's annual Day of the Tree. As we explained our plan, the eyes of the youngsters sparkled. They would get a chance to be part of the rebuilding of the broken village of Biram. Each carrying an olive tree sapling, we would march to the village. There we would plant the trees and the children would have a chance to play awhile before we walked back over the hills and home.

The day was February 17, 1979. Many guests had been invited to participate, including the Israeli prime minister, Knesset members (government leaders), the Israeli police and border police and also members of the national and international press. I was disappointed that none of these special people were able to come, but we marched on anyway, singing as we went. As we approached Biram bearing our olive branches, symbols of peace, we were met by armed Israeli soldiers, journalists, and TV cameramen. Barbed wire had been spread in our path, and the soldiers were carrying machine guns.

I motioned to the children to step back and I went on to meet the officer in charge. "What is wrong, sir? Why do you come with machine guns to meet children who carry olive branches? We only want to plant these saplings in Biram."

"No, that is not possible. You must go back. Turn around and no one will be hurt."

I glanced back at the children. They were standing quietly, waving their olive branches, seemingly unafraid of the danger. I prayed silently, "Lord, keep them safe."

The officer went on. "We have received orders from above. You are forbidden to enter the village of Biram."

I spoke to the reporters and soldiers in Hebrew, rather than Arabic, so all would understand. "Your orders from above are very low orders because they have no morality about them. My dear friends, we love you and regret that you hold those machine guns made to threaten, scare, and kill. When you face olive saplings with machine guns, you have no hope for life. You are scared and you scare others. See these Palestinian youngsters who are all carrying an olive sapling, the tree of peace that promises to endure for centuries! The children are relaxed, while you are very tense with machine guns. We shall never give up, but we shall never carry weapons to plant an olive tree and obtain our human rights to home and freedom."

As I spoke to the soldiers, the TV cameras were rolling. They followed us as we turned and marched back across the hills. As we marched, I started to sing our Easter liturgical hymn that speaks of forgiveness and making peace with our fellow humans and with God. Soon the children's voices rang out along with mine. That evening, the TVs of the world gave witness to our encounter with the soldiers and heard me speak.

The next day, one hundred children went with me to Jerusalem to deliver the olive saplings to the Knesset, the government building, and the officials who worked there. Again, we were refused. I had imagined this would happen so we had brought along small stamped and addressed cartons that had been given to us by the Committee of Biram. The children and I carefully packed each sapling in a carton and took them to the main post office to be mailed to Prime Minister Menachem Begin,

Knesset members, and many other Israeli officials. No one responded to the gift of peace in the form of an olive branch. We were not surprised.

Peace seemed so far away when every day of life was so full of danger. I remembered our summer camp the year before. There were over a thousand children camped in tents near Ibillin. The camp was in the olive grove and the children were bursting with excitement. About noon, thirty armed Israeli soldiers came and asked to inspect the camp. They walked around the olive grove and watched as the children joyfully played games or read in the temporary library. Then the soldiers drove off.

Shortly after they had left, some of the boys discovered a strange little box lying on the ground. Soon, other children spotted similar boxes. We agreed that the boxes had not been there before the soldiers arrived. I sensed danger and quickly assembled the youngsters in a far corner of the camp, where no boxes had been seen. I left them in the care of their counselors and hurried to a nearby gas station to telephone the police.

The police came immediately and carefully removed the strange boxes. They were surprised to find that the thousand people who had been reported to be camped in the olive grove near Ibillin were not Palestinian terrorists but Palestinian children. We never knew if those boxes were bombs or not, but the fear we all experienced was not soon forgotten.

I knew that these precious children, who meant so much to the future of our people, must get the education they needed to bring hope to their lives. Bishop Raya was right. I must build a school. How, I didn't know, but with God's help, it would be done. Day after day I prayed to My Champion, Jesus, searching for a way to fulfill this persistent dream of building a secondary school for the young people of Ibillin.

As the story of the Palestinian tragedy began to reach the eyes and ears of the people around the world, through newspapers and TV coverage, I was asked more and more to travel abroad and speak about our situation. From time to time I spent extended periods abroad, teaching in colleges and universities. Although these trips involved time away from my ever increasing responsibilities, I soon realized that God was opening the door to international help for our building project. And so I spoke of our dream of a secondary school. Financial help was promised from many new friends around the world. One of these new friends was Queen Beatrix of the Netherlands. Because of her influence and that of her prime minister, three men were sent from the Inter-Church Coordination Committee, a Christian group in the Netherlands. This group agreed to give us the money needed for building materials. The actual construction would be done by our own people.

The next step was to apply to the Israeli government for a building permit. The sad thing was that usually Palestinians were either denied a permit, or it took years before one was received. We planned to build immediately. Our friends from the Netherlands had come to visit, and together we had gone over the blueprints for the school. A rocky hillside, called the Mount of the Ogre, had been decided on as the building site. This land, of about five thousand square meters, had been given to the Melkite church many, many years before by one of the church families. It had been in the possession of the church for over three hundred years.

I applied for the building permit in April of 1981. Two weeks later I received word that the permit was refused. "Why?" I asked. The answer was that the building was too expensive, and the proposed land was only for agricultural use. Both of these reasons were not true.

I went to our new bishop for help. Instead of help, I was met by angry accusations. He felt I was wrong to go against the Israeli government by demanding a permit to build an unnecessary school. He was also angry that I had often spoken out against the Israeli government in my travels abroad. In his anger, he said my salary would probably be affected because I refused to stay within the church and preach God's word as a priest was called to do.

His sharp words increased my impatience. I knew I was called to fight for the rights of my people and also to live, as well as preach, God's word. I told the bishop that the salary he paid me would not be needed at all if I could not be free to do God's will. I would rely on the support of the people of my parish. I shook with rage as I stalked out of the office. We had counted on our bishop's support, but just as Mother Josephate had decided so many years before, we must follow a higher authority—God.

In the midst of all of the problems about school construction, word came from Father, who still lived in Gish, that Mother had died peacefully in her sleep. The nuns and I had just visited my parents a short while before and Mother, at the age of eighty, had seemed as vigorous as ever. Now she was gone. All that I had learned about faith, I had learned from my dear parents. They were true reflections of God's love, and through their prayers had helped shape the lives of their children. We knew that Mother now was safe in the arms of her Lord. Her body was buried in Biram, where none of us had been allowed to return. Father then moved to Haifa, at the age of eighty-two, to be with his children. In April of 1989, he went to be with his Lord, and now rests beside Mother on the hillside in Biram.

13

NO BUILDING PERMITS
for PALESTINIANS

We began construction in January of 1982 without the building permit. I had been warned that at any time Israeli tanks may roll up our hill and level the construction site. This was the usual consequence for building without a permit. By the second week in March, the building's steel frame was up and the ground floor was completed. Then it happened. The police roared up and demanded to see me.

"Where is your building permit?"

"I don't have one."

"Then I must arrest you and all of your workers."

"But sir, they are all volunteers. Take me only, as I am the one who is responsible."

"No. We will only take your workers. I have been told that if I take you, the international press will be called into action. We don't want that."

Thirty volunteer construction workers were taken to the police station for questioning and released hours later. This process continued for two months. Four separate groups of workers were arrested. The largest group was made up of seventy-five men.

As the police had planned, fear was now beginning to replace

the enthusiasm of building a school. The nuns and I kept praying for strength and wisdom to break through this wall of fear
and complete the project. We had promised our people the
school would be ready for students in September of 1982.
"Lord, help us keep that promise."

Shortly after Easter, the police chief of all Galilee roared
into the village in his official car. He stopped at my door. I received him in my new living room in the parish house. He demanded that we stop building at once. Of course, I refused. He
threatened to arrest me. When I still refused, he threatened to
arrest the whole village.

"Go ahead, do it. I will bring international volunteers to
help," was my reply.

The police chief stormed out of my living room and was
gone.

I was still shaking from the confrontation. "Now what,
Lord?" As always, into my confusion and powerlessness an answer came. All I needed to do was follow through.

A week later, I placed an anonymous call to the police station to report that the disobedient priest in Ibillin was still not
obeying orders. He had a crew of international volunteers and
the school was still being built. This was true. We had been able
to arrange for eighteen young people to come from Switzerland
for a few weeks to help with construction.

When the police arrived the next day to arrest the volunteers, I asked why they wanted to arrest Swiss citizens who were
only trying to be helpful? The police looked confused. These
blonde young people were certainly not Arabs. They began to
question the young foreigners who, as instructed, told of their
parents' professions rather than their own names. Their fathers
were lawyers and professors, and their mothers were journalists
and government officials.

The police quickly decided that arresting these volunteers
was not a good idea. The police vans left as quickly as they had
come. Several days later, I received a letter saying that my case
would be decided in court in another two weeks. At least the

school was safe for two more weeks. "Thank you, Lord."

Two weeks later, dressed in my priest's clothes, I appeared in court. I tried to impress upon the judge the importance of a school for the children of Ibillin. I also mentioned that so many international friends were involved with the school that it would be a shame if the newspapers got word that the government of Israel had blown up a school just because no building permit had been received. I asked for additional time to hire a lawyer to plead our case. Five months were granted.

I was overjoyed. In five months the school would be completed and students would be in the classrooms. Thanks to God's help and the persistence of His people, the school was opened on September 1, 1982, with five teachers and ninety-two students. It was named Prophet Elias High School in honor of the Prophet Elijah, who dared to speak out against the evil of his day nearly three thousand years ago. I too had been named after Elijah.

Mr. Shmueli, director general of the Ministry of Education, was then invited to see this miracle school. Two years before he had told me it was not humanly possible to construct a school on that hill, now renamed the Mount of Light. He was right, of course, but he had not considered the power of God. Now, he needed to inspect the school and its program to determine how much financial support the Israeli government was required to give us. His decision was based on a careful evaluation ranging from 0 to 100 points. The greater the number, the greater the amount of financial help. He decided on 91.4, which was much higher than most schools in Israel.

My day in court came. All of our funds had gone toward the school so, rather than hire a lawyer, I defended our cause. The Israeli government stated their case: A school had been built without a permit and even though it now had one hundred students, it should be destroyed.

I silently prayed for the words that would solve this dreadful dilemma. Rising to my feet, I faced the judge. "Your honor. You have the power to destroy this building, but you will have to destroy it on the heads of the one hundred Israeli citizens who are learning in that school. If that happens, I will be forced to go all over the world telling what you have done and begging for money to build a new school. I know I could raise millions of dollars, but then I will further stain Israel's reputation, and we don't need that, do we?"

The judge shook his head in dismay. "What is your solution, Father Chacour?"

"There is a simple solution. Give me the building permit. Then the building may remain standing and our children will live to receive a fine education under its roof. I will tell my international friends about the goodness of Israel and the justice of her laws."

I was asked to step into the hall while the judge discussed possible solutions with the government officials. When I returned, the judge announced that they had come to an agreement. I held my breath as I heard his words. "There will be no permit. We will not, however, destroy your school."

This was truly an answer to prayer.

"You know, of course, that operating the school without a permit means no utility service. How will you manage without water?"

"Sir, the village authority has already provided water. That will not change."

"What about electricity?"

"We will have school in the daylight hours and, if needed, we will use kerosene lamps. I guess we will also continue to use the electric cable that is connected to a nearby house."

"What about a telephone?"

"We have the Arabic telephone, mouth to mouth, and that always works well. I have a phone in the parish house which only works about three days a month. We will manage."

I left the courtroom with joy in my heart that our dream had been fulfilled. When I had been brought low with the discouraging turn of events, I was sustained by prayer and the unshakable faith of the children and families in our village. Our path was still not an easy one, and whenever the students would complain about dragging that electric cable from the second floor to the fourth and then back to the first, I would remind them, "You do not have electricity because you do not have a permit. You do not have a permit because you are Palestinian. Just remember: whenever you have the upper hand over any person or any group, Jew or Palestinian, do not use the same methods that are used against you. It is so ugly, so corrupting, to the one who is oppressive." Then I would help them drag the heavy cable.

14

HELP *from* ABROAD

The number of students rapidly grew from 100 to beyond 350, which was the capacity of the existing building. New students kept applying and we did everything possible so they would not be turned away. By 1986 we had crowded nearly 800 students into our small classrooms. More and more students wanted to attend. Building again was a frightening thought but that seemed to be the only way. As I prayed for guidance, I remembered our faithful God who stood beside us as we planned and built the present school. We had to try.

I carefully prepared the papers that the Israeli government required for a building permit. When these papers were presented, I was assured by the government official that it would take three to four months, due to bureaucracy. Bureaucracy or not, I knew we needed to begin so we would be ready for students when school opened in the fall. We started building without the permit.

God's power, along with our prayers and those of our many international friends, could be seen as the new building—a gymnasium—began to take shape. Things were going along well when, in 1987, the order came to stop building and I received a summons to go to court. We stopped and I went to court, in hopes of resolving the problem so we could proceed. Perhaps they would remember the building permit application that was still trapped in the place called *bureaucracy*.

I felt God's presence as I stood before the judge. "Why are you building a gymnasium when you have no building permit, Mr. Chacour?" His sharp words showed no hint of respect for God or the position of a priest.

"Your Honor, our permit application was submitted to you nearly a year ago. I was told it would take three to four months. Our students need more space and we could wait no longer."

"Mr. Chacour, do you realize the consequences of building without a permit? We will be forced to close the school and destroy this illegal gymnasium."

"Sir, Prophet Elias High School has brought hope to our young people. By destroying their school, this hope for a promising future will be gone. Then the Israeli government will need to build prisons for hopeless Palestinian youth. Is this what you want, Your Honor?"

There was silence as the judge weighed my words. "I will review your permit application. Meanwhile, building must stop. Return to this courtroom in six months and we will continue our discussion."

This was good news and bad news. With the judge's promise to review our permit, I felt a sense of hope, but complying with his demand to stop building brought me to my knees yet again. "Where will we find help this time, Lord?"

My prayers continued as I fulfilled my duties as school administrator. Each morning my hope was renewed as I watched hundreds of eager young people make their way down the hills toward the school, books under their arms. As they came, the sounds of classical music were piped out across the village. I greeted the students in the courtyard and shared a thought for the day from my morning reading of scripture. Then, with the music in their hearts and God's word in their minds, they went on to their crowded classrooms.

Students in the courtyard

Unfinished gymnasium

For the time being, all visible progress on our building stopped. Underground, however, construction continued as we dug into the rock beneath the building. In this way three more classrooms were constructed to ease the strain of over-crowded space. Quality education was essential. By fulfilling the demand for students who were well-educated in the field of technology, we would put our youth on an equal plane with Israeli students with whom they were competing for jobs.

In six months I returned to court as directed, in hopes that the desired permit would be granted. Instead, the court hearing was again postponed for six months. I chuckled as I began to record the date on my calendar. It was a Sunday. No priest is required to work or go to court on a Sunday. When brought to the judge's attention, he set a new date, six months into the future. It was also a Sunday. In this way my hearing was put off for a total of six years. This Israeli bureaucracy is not so bad after all.

I kept praying for a solution to this dilemma. At the same time, I kept knocking on the doors of Israeli officials, begging for the needed building permit.

My prayers continued, and one day, while reading the newspaper, I found my answer. It seemed that the new United States Secretary of State, Jim Baker, was upsetting President Bush because he refused to have security guards around his residence. "This situation was meant for me," I thought. Americans, just like Israelis, Palestinians, and all others, were born babies, human beings, children of God. As a human being, perhaps Mr. Secretary of State Jim Baker would be sympathetic to our need and be willing to help.

Before many days, I was on a flight to the United States, Washington, D.C. in particular. I had decided to bring the plight of Prophet Elias High School to the steps of the U. S. government. Perhaps they were more reasonable than our Israeli government.

I knocked on the door of Jim Baker's home. His wife Susan answered and I introduced myself as "another man from Galilee" who hoped to speak to her husband. He was not at home but Susan graciously invited me in and listened to my story.

"What can we do to help you, Father Chacour?"

"Please ask your husband to write a letter to Ytzhak Shamir, asking him for a building permit for our gymnasium and school." As I left, Mrs. Baker assured me she would do this. Susan Baker wrote the letter, and when her husband returned, she asked him to sign it so it could be sent to Shamir. His reply was, "No, I will not sign and send this letter. Instead, I will take it to Mr. Shamir along with copies of Father Chacour's two books: *Blood Brothers* and *We Belong to the Land*." Within a few weeks the letter was delivered by both Susan and Jim Baker.

Since that visit, Susan Baker and I have become prayer partners and close friends. We prayed together on the phone, and she often called me when her husband was on a mission of peace for our country. She would ask me to call some of my friends, imploring them to pray for the success of this peace mission on behalf of the Palestinians.

A short time later, the building permit was granted and we were officially able to continue building. Gone was the threat of having our building destroyed by bulldozers. When Mr. Perez visited the school later, he said, "Father Chacour, Israel has tried to find the enemy in you for twenty years and we have failed. We have found only a friend. Because of this friendship, I would like to be an ambassador for your school."

I thanked him kindly for his offer and then boldly asked, "Do you plan to be a good or a less-good ambassador?"

"I will do all I can to be a good ambassador." Mr. Perez was true to his word. He was an excellent ambassador for the Prophet Elias High School.

One and a half years later Jim and Susan Baker came to visit the school. They were amazed at the progress. The visit was not to see me, but it was their way to show solidarity with their Palestinian Christian brothers and sisters and to see for themselves how God had answered our prayers. Plans were now in progress to grow beyond the secondary school to a junior college. Since my visit to the Bakers' home, we have continually been blessed by God's power at work through prayer.

Interior of the new gymnasium

15

FROM SOLDIERS *to* PEACEMAKERS

We began the year 1994 bright with hope. As we realized our need to go beyond a secondary school, we started making space to expand as a junior college. Through the years the international community, as well as many church bodies, have been very involved in our plans. What joy we felt on March 10 when the new gymnasium was filled with 2,400 guests along with the students and staff of the Mar Elias Community College. On that very special occasion I was presented with the World Methodist Council's 1994 Peace Award. It was with deep humility that I accepted this award on behalf of all of those who had worked so hard to make our educational dreams a reality.

Our college had students who were Christians, Muslims, Druze and Jews. These young people were not only receiving technological training in the fields of Business Administration, Civil Engineering, Surveying and Landscape Architecture, Computer Programming, Air Conditioning/Acclimatization, Printing/Offset-Montage, Chemistry and Food Engineering (Catering), Media and Communications, and Academic Upgrading for Teachers but they were learning to work together to build a peaceful society. God is always true to God's promises to provide even more than we ask or think.

The first building needed for the college was a library. We

pushed ahead to have that ready for the beginning of school in September. Then we were able to divide the old library into three classrooms. We reduced the number of secondary school students by 100, so the college was able to begin with 100 students. We had plans to enroll up to 1,500 students in the future. To accommodate this number, we needed about thirty-eight additional classrooms.

At first, our college was not recognized by the Israeli government, and for that reason we did not receive any subsidies (financial aid). Of course, teachers had to be paid, so I went to my friends in the international community and begged for financial help to pay these salaries. The sales of my books were all used for that purpose, too.

Then one day we had a call from the office of the Foreign Minister, Shimon Perez. He had recently received the Nobel Peace Prize and wanted to give his first peace lecture at our school. What an opportunity for us to share our hospitality with an official of the Israeli government. About 1,600 people came to hear him.

Two months later the Minister of Education came with a present—a very valuable gift. To us it was more valuable than money. He came with a certificate of recognition for Mar Elias College and full accreditation. With this recognition came financial help from the government which was absolutely essential to fulfill our vision. Taking first place in Hebrew Studies in 1993 had been but a beginning as we worked toward this goal of accreditation.

The Minister of Education then asked if we would be willing to accept Jewish students who had completed their service in the army. My reply was emphatic. "Oh please, send us the whole Israeli Army. Along with their academic lessons, they will learn two things: to throw away their weapons and put them in the garbage and then step forward to conquer the hearts of Palestinian children; not with guns but with smiles that express the attitude of the heart for justice, righteousness, peace, and security with respect for all people. They will be treated exactly like all of our other students—no better and no worse. After all, they too are God's precious children, created in God's image."

So far we have only had four former soldiers. I wish with all my heart that we had 40 or 400. We must learn to live with fellow Jews and treat them as equals—not as mini-gods or mini-devils. Fifty years ago the Jew was treated as *dirty Jew*. Now it is the Palestinian who has undeservedly inherited the title of *dirty Arab* or even *terrorist*. All of this is a crime against humanity. Palestinian children in their refugee camps today are no more *dirty terrorists* than the Jewish children were *dirty* in Germany during World War II. Both of these groups have experienced situations in which they are literally terrorized by what is being done to them by others. May the God whom we all serve teach us to live together peacefully.

We were making good progress in Ibillin but all was not well in the rest of Israel/Palestine. There was a suicidal Israeli terrorist attack in Jerusalem and soon after in Tel Aviv. We reacted very strongly, just as we had when a Jewish terrorist had attacked praying Muslims at a mosque in Hebron. He mowed them down as they were prostrated in prayer. In those times we wrote letters to the Israeli prime minister. Our school went on strike to express our outrage for such terrorism, violence and barbarism.

Soon after this, some Palestinian brothers and sisters, who had lost all hope in life and in human beings, decided to blow themselves up, killing as many others as they could inside buses in Israel, in Hadera, in Jerusalem and the last in Tel Aviv. This was so horrible! We could not believe that human beings could commit such a crime. We wrote to the Israeli prime minister, expressing our solidarity with every Jew in the world. It is a scandal when anyone commits such a crime.

While discussing these acts of terrorism with my students in the college, one of them said, "Abuna, we must do more than write letters. Anyone can write a letter. I am willing to donate blood for the wounded Jews in Tel Aviv." Another student said she would do that, too. As a priest and educator, I felt I also must do the same. Within a half hour the entire student body decided to do this.

I called the Jewish hospital in Haifa and asked them to send some nurses to take our blood. Those at the hospital believed what I said. They did not send one nurse. They sent fifteen Jewish nurses with all the equipment to pump our blood.

I was afraid that only ten or fifteen students would donate blood and that would not be enough to show our solidarity. I was amazed to see that the nurses had to work from 8:00 in the morning to 2:30 in the afternoon pumping our blood. Out of the 350 adult students in the college, 300 of them lined up to give their life blood for wounded Jewish brothers and sisters in Tel Aviv.

I will never forget the moment I laid down to donate my blood. Beside me lay a Druze teacher, next to him a Jewish teacher, and beside her an American volunteer. We all gave our blood as an example for our students. That evening, March 8, 1996, I was able to say on the TV and in the newspaper, "I am so proud that today there is Palestinian blood flowing in Jewish veins. I hope you all discover that we have the same blood, the human blood. We pray this will be the last time anyone will have to donate blood for injured people, Jews or Palestinians, who have been hurt in terrorist acts."

Two weeks later the Israeli government, under the leadership of Shimon Perez, bombed a U.N. refugee camp in Cana, southern Lebanon. The bombs were made in the United States. Several hundred refugees were killed and many more were wounded. These people too were children of Abraham and created in the image and likeness of God. We were broken once more by this terrible act. We kept this wound in our hearts as we realized again that our government is ruled by the idea that might is right, which totally goes against the laws of God. We found comfort in our faith and knew that the last word will not be in might, arrogance or human blindness. The last word will be with God.

16

REFUSAL *to* GIVE UP

Once more I presented myself before the Minister of Interior Affairs to obtain a building permit. Our new building would house fifty-three classrooms, as we took steps toward expanding to a four-year university. Our application had been sent nine months before and once more it was stuck in that place called *bureaucracy*.

I knew that all of our papers were absolutely in order so I decided to play the big game. I went in person to the Ministry of Interior Affairs where building permits are to be given. When I entered the office of the president I asked, "Do you have coffee for me?" He ordered that for me but then I added, "You should also order breakfast."

"We will do that gladly for you, Father Chacour."

I said, "What about lunch and dinner?"

"Why?" he asked incredulously.

"Because, I plan to stay here the whole time, and within two or three hours I will have guests here also."

"Who will that be?"

"My teachers. We'll start first by bringing the Jewish teachers to join me in your office. Two by two they will come, each half hour until we have all 181 teachers joining us here. They will stay forever or until we have the permit." He did not take me seriously till one half hour later, when the first two Jewish teachers arrived. They started asking me, "What about the building permit? Will you get it or will we have to sleep here tonight? We are not going home until you get the permit." Then two others came and then two more.

Finally, the president saw that we were very serious. He said to me, "Father Chacour, we will give you the permit. Come back tomorrow and everything will be ready."

"I don't need to come back or go away. I'll stay here till tomorrow. I am very happy here. Don't worry." I started reading and my teachers were sitting around me reading as well. The officer went out and twenty minutes later he was back again.

"Father Chacour, we will give you the permit but go and bring some money to pay for the permit, because you have to pay the fees."

I said, "How much is it?"

"3,400 shekels," he answered (almost $1,000).

"Well, I don't need to go away. I have the money here."

"We can't convince you of anything. You will have what you want."

"Exactly. I am determined this time to stay here—even if it's one year. I want this permit in my hands. It is enough that we despise each other. I respect you so much that you have to respect yourself and give us the permit."

He said, "I don't know. What can I do?"

"Do whatever you can."

He left again and was back in one half hour. "Where is the money?" he said.

"This is the money," and I gave it to him.

He went away and came back with the permit. Now, we are building with a permit for the first time.

Our new building will have four floors. We want to provide dormitory facilities for female students. Dormitories are not as essential for boys as they can come and go more easily in Israeli society. We are hoping that by the year 2000 we will have the first Christian University in the Galilee and even be able to offer Ph.D's in several fields. Then, perhaps, Palestinians who have gone abroad to teach will want to return to Israel/Palestine to finish out their teaching career. Mar Elias University will be an excellent way to build bridges to other Arab countries also.

I am happy to say that our relations with the Israeli Ministry of Education and that of Welfare and Labor are very good right now, so we are making considerable progress toward fulfilling our dream. We have opened a Center for Religious Pluralism and our first lecture series was "Abraham the Father of the Believers in Jewish, Christian, and Muslim Traditions." This was a series of five lectures given by Dr. Paul Treat from the United States and me. We are preparing for a new series of lectures: "Isaiah the Man, the Prophet, the School" and "Isaiah the Message in Both Christian and Jewish Traditions."

In spite of the turmoil in our government, we must forge ahead toward peace. Our students are mainly Israeli citizens, with a few from the West Bank and Jordan. We all must make a positive investment toward a brighter future where peace and justice for all people will be the rule by which we live. In the 1997-1998 school year we will be in partnership with the Technion Institute in Haifa, and we also have strong ties with the Tel Aviv University. The school's future looks very promising.

The story of how God has worked miracles in Ibillin is being spread around the world through my books: *Blood Brothers* and *We belong to the Land*. I have been invited to speak at colleges and universities in Australia, Europe and the United States. Volunteers from these countries spend time helping at the school in various capacities. We have sent students from the school to visit in communities abroad, staying with local families and attending school. They stay for a few days or up to several months.

God will continue to work through willing people in order to accomplish great things. This will happen in spite of governments or people who are not willing to share what really belongs to God—this holy land called Israel/Palestine. Someday the world will be able to see the bright side of welcome, and people will come from near and far to see the evidence of God's plan at work in the land that three faiths claim as home: Israel/Palestine.

EPILOGUE

Things are changing in Israel, both for Palestinians and Jews. That change began with a handshake. In September of 1993, Yassar Arafat, the Palestinian leader, and Yitzhak Rabin, the Israeli Prime Minister, participated in that historic handshake which took place on the White House lawn, right in Washington, D.C. With this handshake, both of the leaders agreed to honor the existence of the other group of people, as well as their right to live peacefully in Israel.

This was an exciting beginning to a complicated peace agreement which will take a long while to develop. But, it was a beginning, and most people in Israel celebrate that beginning. In this agreement, each side has been asked to give up much, as initially they each wanted to hold exclusive claim to the Holy Land and not allow the other group to live there at all. There are still some extremist factions on each side of the issue who, even now, think that the old idea is the best.

One achievement the Palestinians have gained is the right to raise their flag, which up to the time of the peace accord could not be legally flown. For Palestinians it signaled the start of a new era of hope. Palestinians were now called on to move forward to achieve peace for all peoples who share the land. The temptation was to cling to a record of abuses and play the victim. Acting with that type of negative attitude does not exhibit Christ's love and forgiveness. Both Jews and Palestinians have suffered greatly at the hands of others during this century and before. The time had come to move beyond that suffering and to work together to build a land of peace.

Tragedy struck the nation, however, when on November 4, 1995, Yitzhak Rabin was assassinated as he left a peace rally in Tel Aviv. His assassin was Yigal Amir who had been raised as an Orthodox Jew. Amir believed that Israel was for Jews only and as Rabin began to move the government away from this idea toward a peace agreement with Palestinians, Amir's anger erupted into violence. Shimon Perez was selected as Prime Minister to fulfill Rabin's term of office. Elections were held in May of 1996 and Benjamin Netanyahu was elected, defeating Perez by a narrow margin. Since then, progress toward peace has slowed considerably, as Jewish settlements have expanded on land illegally confiscated from Palestinians. More violence erupted in March 1997 when the hillside called Jabel Abu Gneim was cleared to make way for the settlement Har Homa. It seems that violence will continue until both Palestinians and Israelis have equal access to peace and security and the rights of each group are honored.

Changes came to the village of Ibillin, too. The school that Abuna Chacour established in 1981 had 82 students who studied in the newly constructed community center. Today there is a kindergarten with 178 children, a secondary school (high school) with 1800 students, and a community college with 650 students. The school campus has also grown and now includes a gymnasium (which was begun in 1986 but was not completed until 1992 due to more complications with building permits) and a library which was completed in 1994. In that year the secondary school expanded to include a junior college.

Gymnasium and library

Continuing construction

The students' ages range from fourteen to thirty-five and include young people from the four main faiths in Israel: Christianity, Judaism, Islam and Druze (a religion that follows a blend of Islam, Christianity and paganism). Teachers on the staff represent all four of these faith groups. There are also many international students, mainly from Europe and the United States.

Abuna Chacour believes that by working together these people of different faiths can help achieve a lasting peace in Israel. It won't be easy, but those involved with Mar Elias Community College and Secondary School and the people of Ibillin are determined to do their part to make this dream a reality.

LIVING STONES

Living stones in a holy land;
    listening, living, gently giving
        love to all who enter in.
"Welcome" is the word they say.
    Peace they yearn for every day.
Yet fear grips every heart and home
    as guns and tanks create a tomb
        where hope is often buried deep.
For some it even seems to sleep.
    Christ's miracles live on today
        as gentle spirits kneel to pray,
        rejecting hate and guns and war,
        looking to God as in days of yore.
He alone real peace will bring
    as shepherds and angels join to sing
        "Alleluia to our King!"

—Sue Ellen Johnson

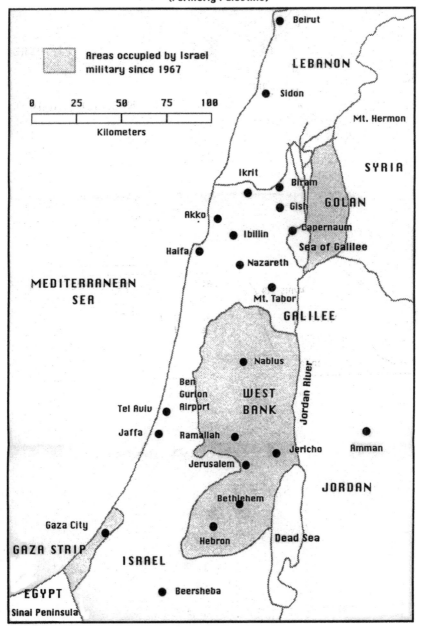

Israel
(Formerly Palestine)

CHRONOLOGY CHART

2200 B.C.	Abraham born: father of Jews, Muslims, and Christians
7 B.C.	Jesus Christ born
27-30 A.D.	Christ's ministry
30 A.D.	Christ's death and resurrection
47-60 A.D.	Paul's missionary journeys and imprisonment
325 A.D.	Church conference: Council of Nicea
570 A. D.	Birth of Mohammed: founder of Islam
1200-1400 A.D.	The Crusades
1897 A.D.	Birth of Zionism
1914-1918 A.D.	World War I
1917 A. D.	Balfour Declaration
1922 A. D.	League of Nations begins
1939-1945 A.D.	World War II: Hitler and Nazis come to power in Germany
	Holocaust: period of extermination of 6,000,000 Jews
1947 A.D.	United Nations Partition
1948 A. D.	State of Israel born May 14 David Ben Gurion, Premier
1948 A.D.	First Arab/Israeli War
1948 A.D.	Biram and Ikrit occupied by Zionists
1950 A.D.	Zionists begin kibbutzes
1955 A.D.	Gaza invaded by Zionist forces
1956 A.D.	Suez Canal crisis
1969 A.D.	Golda Meir becomes Israel's fourth Prime Minister

BIBLIOGRAPHY

Ateek, Naim Stifan. *Justice, and Only Justice.* Maryknoll, N.Y.: Orbis Books, 1991.

Chacour, Elias. Lectures and interviews. 1994-1997.

Chacour, Elias, w/David Hazard. *Blood Brothers.* Grand Rapids: Chosen Books, 1983.

Chacour, Elias. Lectures and tapes. 1992-1997.

Chacour, Elias, w/Mary Jensen. *We Belong to the Land.* San Francisco: Harper & Row, 1991.

Chapman, Colin. *Whose Promised Land, Israel or Palestine?* Oxford, England: Lion Publishing, 1992.

Kimball, Charles. *Angle of Vision.* New York: Friendship Press, 1992.

O'Neill, Dan and Don Wagner. *Peace or Armageddon? The Unfolding Drama of the Middle East Peace Accords.* Grand Rapids: Zondervan, 1993.

ORDER FORM

SUE ELLEN JOHNSON
P. O. Box 495
Union, WA 98592-0495
(360) 898-8407

DATE:_____

From: _____
_____
_____
_____

Contact person _____
Phone _____ Fax _____
E-mail _____

QUANTITY	DESCRIPTION	UNIT PRICE	AMOUNT
	THE OTHER SIDE OF WELCOME Sue Ellen Johnson 1-880222-30-2	$10.00	
	SUBTOTAL		
	SALES TAX (8%, WA residents only)		
	S & H (1-2 books $2.00, 3-5 $2.50, 6-7 $3.00, 8-10 $3.50; Priority 1-5 $3.50)		
	TOTAL		

THANK YOU FOR YOUR ORDER!

The author is available for speaking engagements. Please contact the author at the above address or phone number.

If you wish to donate a gift of money to Father Chacour's Mar Elias Secondary School and Junior College, the foundation address is as follows: Pilgrims of Ibillin, 16 Lakeshore Drive, Grosse Pointe Farms, MI 48236.